numbers

a book by John J. Reiss

Bradbury Press • Scarsdale, N.Y.

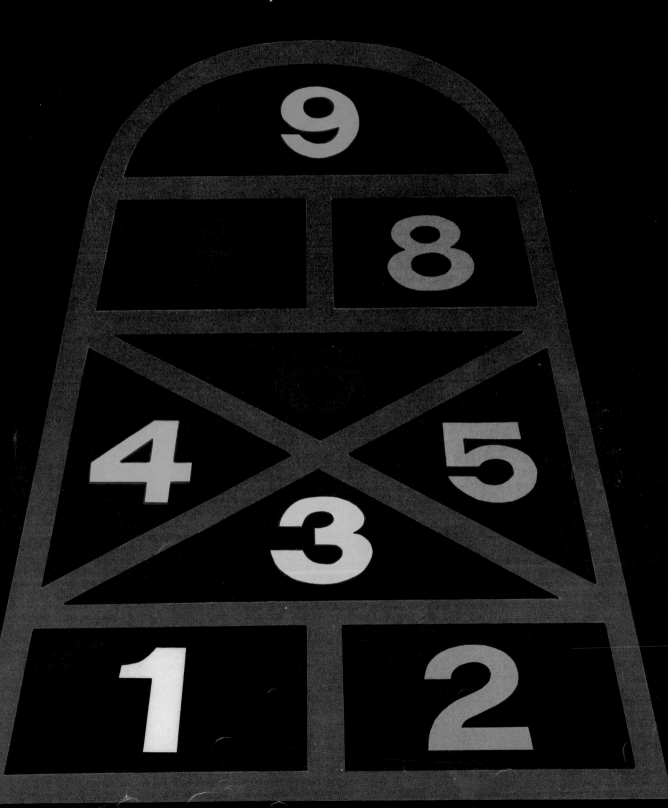

Library of Congress Catalog Card Number: 76-151313
Manufactured in the United States of America
ISBN 0-87888-029-1
The typeface used in this book is Helvetica.
The illustrations, composed of forms cut
from colored glazed papers, are reproduced
in full color.

5 6 7 8 9   81 82 83 84 85

To Kenny Brown and Meg Moynihan

one 1 boy

socks

2

two

shoes

clover leaf

traffic lights

3

three

4 four

legs

wheels

starfish arms

five 5

six **6**

birthday candles

horse-chestnut leaf

7

seven

ravens

eight 8 reindeer

nine **9**

baseball players

houses

ten 10

toes

kites

eleven 11

twelve

12

hours

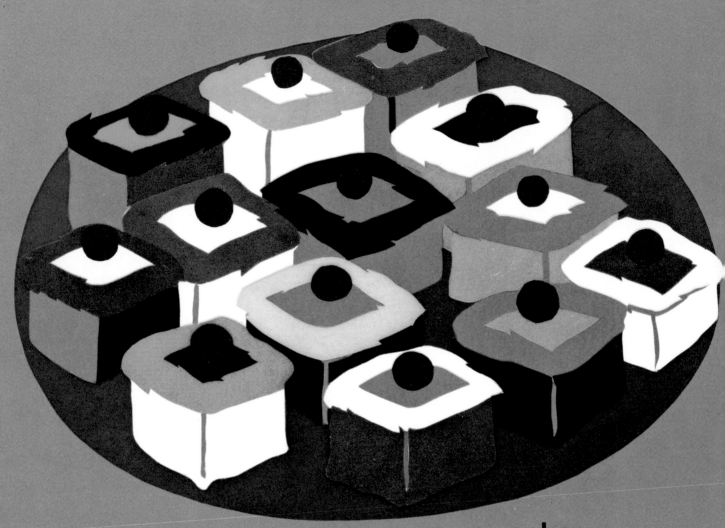

cakes

13

thirteen

14

fourteen

bananas

grapefruit

15

fifteen

16
sixteen
pigeons

marbles

17

seventeen

18

eighteen

crayons

radishes

19
nineteen

20
&
twenty

portholes

thirty**30**

fingers

flowers

forty

40

fifty

50

candy kisses

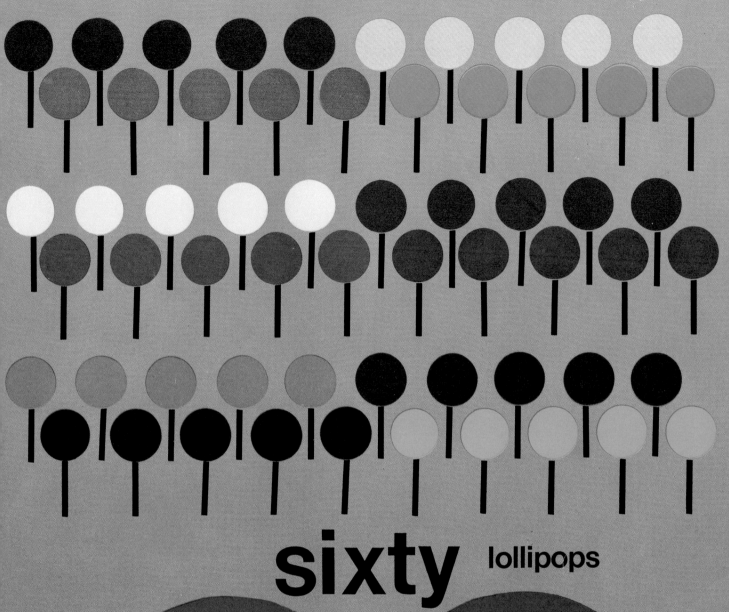

sixty lollipops

seventy

beads

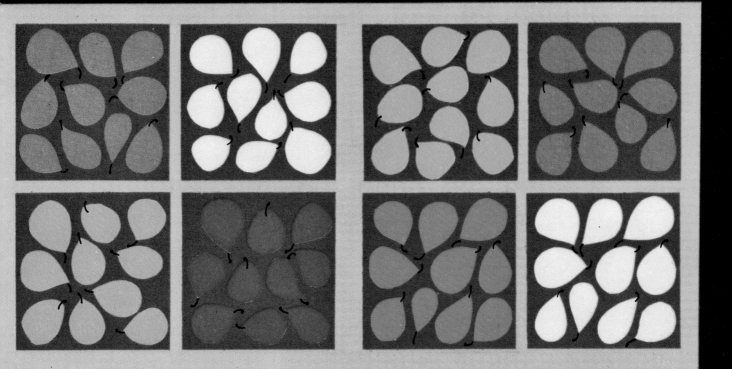

pears

eighty

90

ninety

gumballs

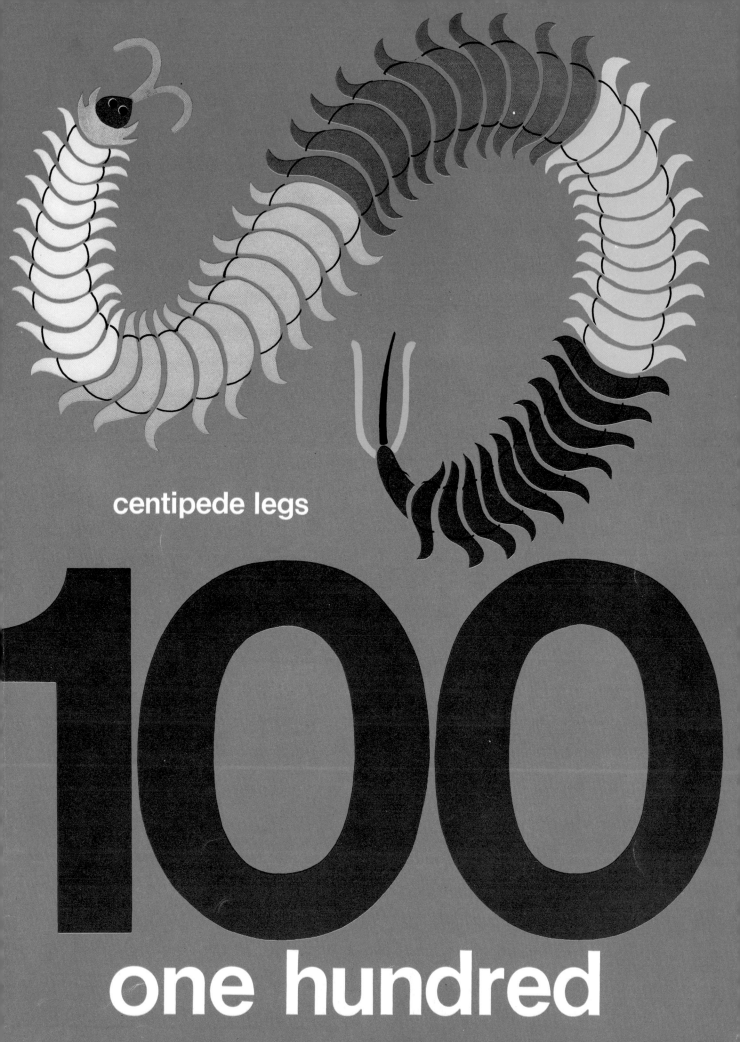

centipede legs

100
one hundred

one thousand
1000

raindrops